3rd Edition

by Doug DuBosque

Growing books for growing people!

For my brother Rick, who encouraged
my car enthusiasm at an early age,
without revealing how to work the
clutch on his Triumph TR-4.

Copyright ©1993-2015 Douglas C. DuBosque.
All rights reserved.
Published by Peel Productions, Inc.
Vancouver, Washington, USA

Draw Cars 3rd edition

ISBN 10: 0-939217-37-6

ISBN-13: 978-0-939217-37-3

Cataloging-in-Publication Data (2nd edition, 1997)

DuBosque, D. C.
　　Draw Cars / by Doug DuBosque
　　　　p.　　cm.
　　Summary: provides step-by-step instructions for drawing popular cars,
including racing cars, exotics, and off-road vehicles.
　　ISBN
　　1. Automobiles in art--Juvenile literature. 2. Drawing--technique--Juvenile
literature. [1. Automobiles in art. 2. Drawing--Technique.] I. Title.
NC825.A8D83 1997
743'.89629222--dc21

　97-25458

Did you know?

You can find frequently-updated
reference material (photos) and
inspiration on our Pinterest feed.
Check it out at:

drawbooks.com/drawcars

Distributed to the trade
and art markets in North America
by F&W Media

(800) 289-0963

DRAW cars

3rd edition

Contents

Getting started

Supplies

Find a comfortable place to draw – with decent light, so you can see what you're doing.

As you start to learn about car designs, shapes and proportions, don't worry too much about materials.

Use a pencil that's longer than your finger. Sharpen it when it gets dull! (The pencil, not your finger.)

If you have colored pencils, use them. In that case, it's best to do the first steps of the drawing with a colored pencil similar to the final color of the vehicle.

Get a separate eraser. My favorite is a kneaded type, available in art supply and craft stores. The eraser on your pencil will disappear quickly, and hard erasers leave "crumbs" on your drawing.

For smooth shading with a soft pencil, consider a tortillon, or blending tool.

For practice drawings, use recycled paper – for example, draw on the back of old photocopies or computer printouts.

Always draw lightly at first, so you can erase problems as you need to.

Save your drawings and learn from them.

Enjoy drawing great cars!

Positive attitude!

Persistence!

Practice!

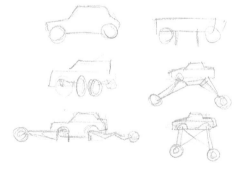

My reference material for the last edition *Draw Cars*. In 1997, even if you could find good photos online, they'd take forever to download because the Internet was so slow.

Reference material

To make a realistic drawing of a car (or anything), you have to look at one. Usually this requires reference material. In this book, the reference material is my drawing, but you can find much more on the Internet.

Do a search for the type of car that interests you, then click "images" instead of "web" in the search results.

I have posted links to the newer editions to this book on our web site:

drawbooks.com/drawcars

Of course, you can use your own photos as well.

A rare Jaguar XKE I spotted in a gas station near my home in Uruguay.

The secrets of drawing

No drawing is perfect. Every time I finish a drawing, I look at it and think, "not perfect, but not bad." I encourage you to approach your drawings in the same way.

Drawing = looking. Most people who "can't" draw simply don't know how to look. I'll show you how to look at a car, take it apart visually, and put it back together on paper.

As your pencil changes, so should your focus. When your pencil is sharp, make fine lines or darken existing lines. As it gets dull, use it to fill dark areas like wheel wells or do shading.

Turn your paper as you draw. Put your thumb and forefinger together. Move your wrist back and forth. This produces a natural curve. Turn your paper to take advantage.

Use a piece of scrap paper under your hand to keep from smudging your drawing.

Use your eraser. The best type is a kneadable artist's eraser, which doesn't leave crumbs on your drawing.

You'll see amazing things in the mirror. As you get to the end of your drawing, look at it in a mirror, or if you can, hold it up to a light and look through the back of the paper. Seriously, this will make a huge difference as you can spot things to correct.

Put the date on your drawing. This will help you appreciate your progress as you produce better drawings.

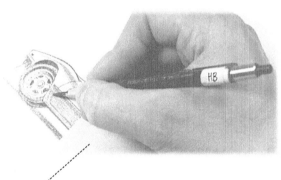

Protective paper keeps drawing clean

Kneadable eraser can be pinched into a point for close work

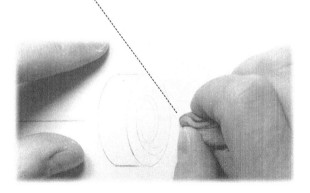

Part one: draw a car from the side

In the next few pages, I'll show you an approach to drawing a car in profile. You'll learn about proportions and key lines, and angles to look for.

Even with the most boxlike vehicles, curves and proportions matter!

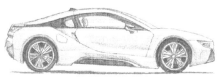

In newer cars, angles and curves present even more of a challenge. So pay attention and follow along the steps of this lesson first, since they will apply to every other car profile.

The basics

Always start your drawing lightly!

As I mentioned, your reference material will be my drawings, but once you understand the basics you can apply them to any car you want to draw.

2015 Toyota Camry

Draw a light horizontal line for the ground. Leave room above it for your car.

Draw a circle for the wheel. Don't worry if it isn't perfectly round at first.

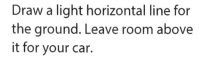

Now measure the diameter of the wheel in your reference material, and see how many wheels fit between the front and the back.

diameter

You can measure like this with your pencil.

On this car, the front and rear wheel are separated by a little over three diameters.

As you'll see in part two, every car is different, so you should always measure.

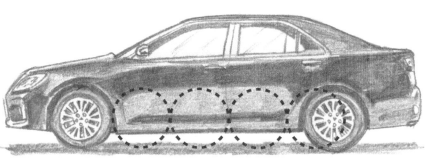

The wheels on this car are separated by a little more than three diameters.

Always start out lightly!

For the drawings in part two, I'll supply a diagram like the one above.

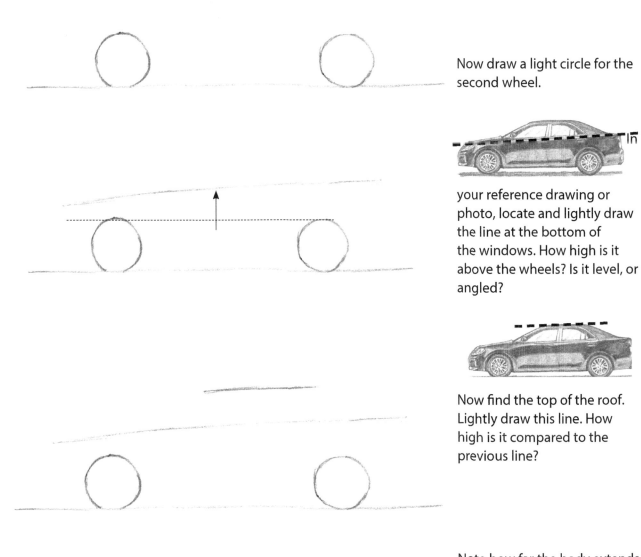

Now draw a light circle for the second wheel.

your reference drawing or photo, locate and lightly draw the line at the bottom of the windows. How high is it above the wheels? Is it level, or angled?

Now find the top of the roof. Lightly draw this line. How high is it compared to the previous line?

Note how far the body extends beyond the front wheel. Lightly sketch the front of the car, and the bottom line to the wheel.

Do the same for the rear end of the vehicle.

Now find the point where the windshield (windscreen) meets the hood (bonnet). Is it above the front wheel? Behind?

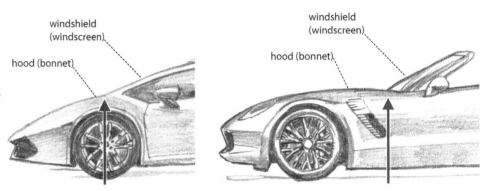

windshield (windscreen)

hood (bonnet)

windshield (windscreen)

hood (bonnet)

In this car, the two meet at the back of the front wheel. Using your wheel measurement, you can now determine where the windshield meets the roof. Draw the windshield line, then the slanted hood.

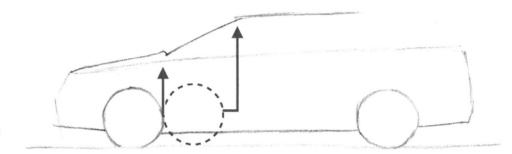

Find the rear end of the roof by comparing it to the rear wheel, and draw the line of the rear window.

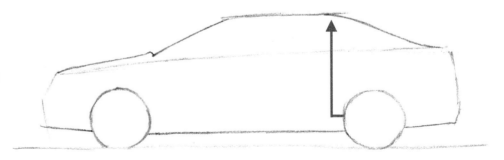

Always start out lightly!

Draw the dark cut-out portion of the body that surrounds the wheels. These dark wheel wells are essential for making your car drawing look real!

Draw the top window line. Look carefully! Add the rear view mirror.

Look at the pillars on this car! The a-pillars hold either side of the windshield in place. B-pillars start where the driver and passenger-side windows end. C-pillars hold the sides of a car's rear window in place. Longer body styles may also have a D pillar.

a-pillar   b-pillar   c-pillar

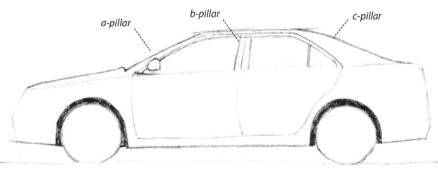

Add a line for trim at the top of the windows, the b-pillar, and the divider in the rear window (can you figure out why it's there? Hint: think about opening the window).

Lightly draw the door outlines. Typically, on a four-door sedan, the front doors are bigger (a coupe has two doors).

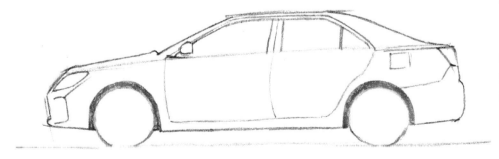

Outline front and rear end shapes: head light, tail light, and other details.

Because the reference material is a photo (not a diagram), the far side of the interior roof shows as a dark area. Add it, and some light lines to make the windows look like glass.

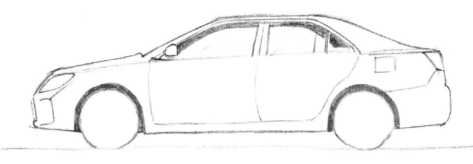

Though I have referred to the round things we drew as wheels, the wheel is actually the metal part (perhaps covered by a plastic hub cap). The outside part is the tire.

Draw two circles for the wheels.

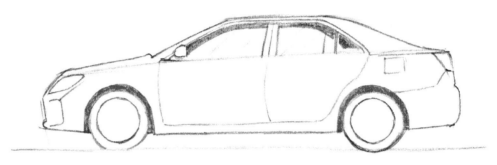

This very complicated wheel design consists of fifteen spokes. Rather than trying to draw each, you can start by drawing the space between them.

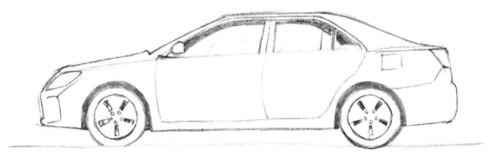

Then you can add the smaller shapes, two dark triangles between each.

(You can also substitute simpler wheels!)

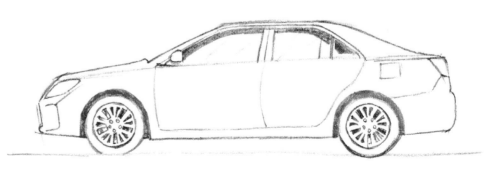

Tips and Tricks: Wheels

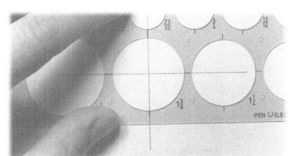

"Aren't wheels always round?" you ask. No, in fact, wheels appear round or elliptical, depending on the angle from which you view them. Round wheels can be both fun and frustrating to draw.

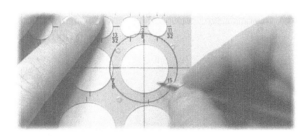

If you want perfect circles, you might want to buy a transparent circle template. Make a horizontal and vertical line, then align them with the marks on the template. Then draw circle after circle, using different size holes in the template.

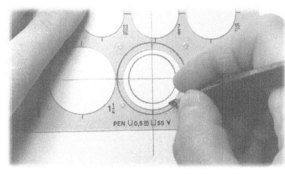

If you don't have a template, turning your paper as you draw will help. Use a piece of scrap paper under your hand so you don't smudge other parts of the drawing.

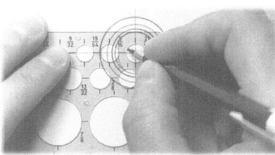

Wheel and hubcap designs range from simple to very complex. In addition to counting the spokes, look at the shape of the negative spaces between them. It may be easier to draw the empty spaces, rather than the spokes themselves.

Left, top to bottom:
0, 3, 4, 5, 5 X 2, 5 X 3, 6

Right: 7 X 2, 11, 12

Once the wheels are complete, add shading for the tires.

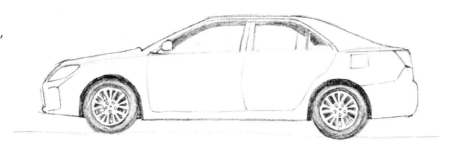

Draw door handles. Make light guide lines for shading the body panels.

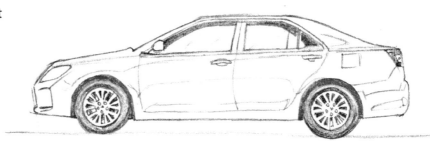

Look carefully at your reference material! Add shading to your drawing. You can smooth it with a tortillon or blending tool (see page 4), and you can use your eraser to add highlights. Spend as much time as you need at this stage.

When your pencil is sharp, go over details and lines. When it gets dull, use it to shade.

Part two: more cars in profile

Lincoln MKC

The 2015 MKC is a crossover vehicle, combining sport utility vehicle features with passenger car comfort.

Start with the ground line, wheel circles, level roof line, and slanting main body line. How far is that line above the rear wheel? Front wheel?

Add window outlines, wheel wells, and side mirror.

Continue to add details, including the wheel rims.

Add shading or color to finish your drawing.

Remember:
- Start out lightly!
- Turn your drawing as you work. Use a piece of scrap paper to keep your hand off finished parts.
- While your pencil is sharp, go over fine details and make lines cleaner. As it gets duller, add shading.
- Clean up any smudges with your eraser. Make sure all final lines are crisp and sharp.

Lamborghini Huracán

Introduced in 2014, the mid-engine, all-wheel-drive Huracán (hurricane in Spanish) has a top speed of 325 km/h (202 mph). That's fast.

Draw the ground line. Using the wheel diagram above, draw the wheels the correct distance apart. Add a line for the bottom of the body, very close to the ground, one for the angled lower window edge, and a short level one for the top of the roof.

Add the rest of the roof top and the rear details. Draw the hood and front end details. Add the mirror and top of the windows.

Note that the door handle is about one wheel diameter forward of the rear wheel. Look carefully at details such as the angles of the front and rear, air scoops, and exhaust pipes.

Add shading or color.

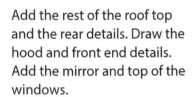

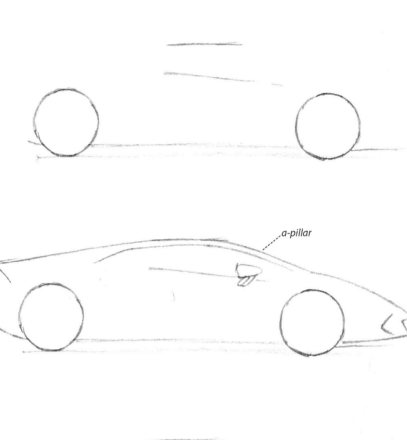

a-pillar

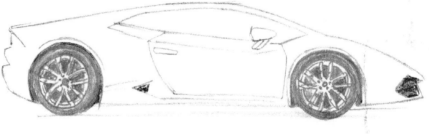

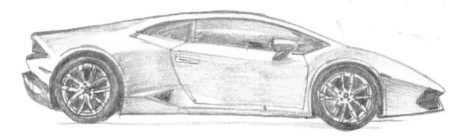

Always start your drawing lightly!

The i8 plug-in hybrid sports car combines a 3-cylinder turbocharged gasoline engine with two electric ones. Its speed is electronically limited to "only" 250 km/h (160 mph).

Draw the ground line. Using the wheel diagram above, draw the wheels the correct distance apart. Make light lines for the roof top, window bottom, and bottom of car.

Add wheel wells, and circles for the wheel rims.

Add another set of circles for the inside of the rim. Make small circles in the center, and divide each wheel into five parts. Add —yikes!—all the other bits and curves you see.

I have simplified the wheels, otherwise very challenging to draw. Add lines on either side of the five you drew, then make little black triangles pointing inward. Add the window outline and details.

Now you're ready to shade or color! Remember to turn your paper as you draw, putting another piece under your hand so you don't smudge your work. Do details with a sharp pencil, and shading when it gets dull.

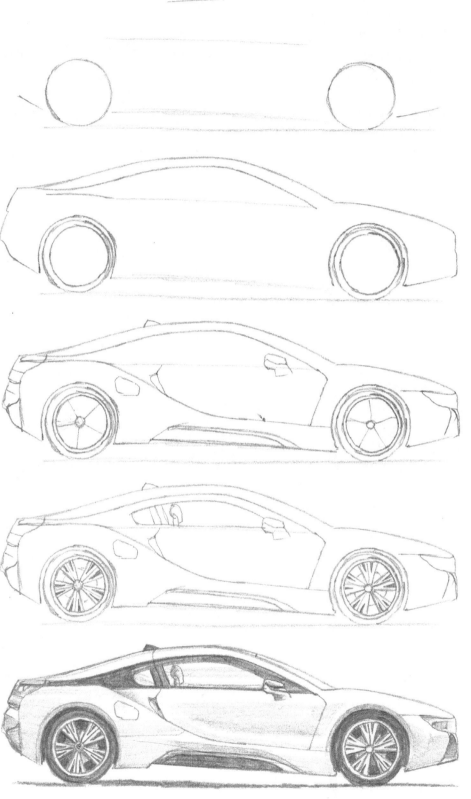

Ferrari 458 Italia

The Ferrari 458 was introduced at the 2009 Frankfurt Auto Show in Germany. It's a two-seater, mid-engine car with a top speed of 325 km/h (202 mph).

Start with the ground line and circles for wheels. Draw a straight line for the bottom of the car, that curves at each end.

Add circles for wheel rims, the mirror, curved line for the bottom of the roof, and details for the front and back.

Add door and body-panel lines and other details. Draw the slightly curved bottom panel. Make circles in the center of each wheel and five lines out to the rims. Remember to draw with the natural way your hand pivots. Notice I was too lazy to turn the paper upside-down for the bottom of the window — and it shows!

Add additional spokes. Notice how I had to erase part of the front wheel. Use your eraser if you need to!

Add shading, using a blending tool (or rolled-up paper towel). Add the dark cast shadow beneath, making it blend into the dark area of the wheel well.

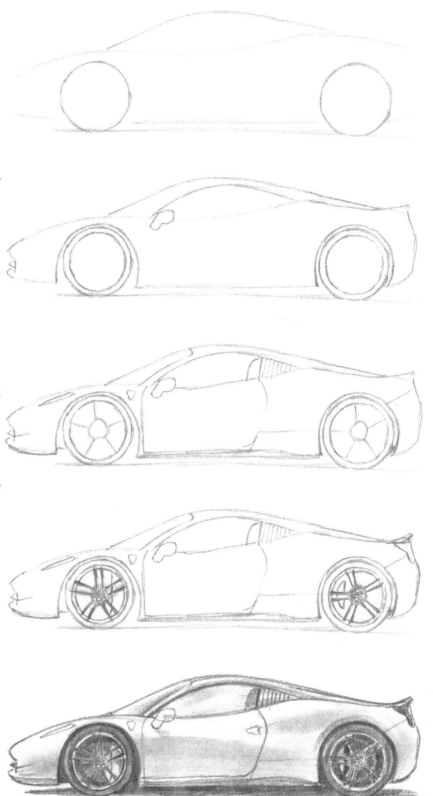

Always start out lightly!

First introduced in 1992, the Viper is now (2015 model year) in its fifth generation, but retains its distinctive look and now features a 600 V10 horsepower engine. The original prototype, from a truck engine, was cast by Lamborghini, which at the time was a subsidiary of Chrysler!

Draw the ground line. Using the wheel diagram above, draw the wheels the correct distance apart. Add lines for the bottom of the car, then others to indicate the bottom and top of the window, and top of the roof.

Complete the curves and angles of the body.

Add wheel wells, basic body lines, and other details. Note how the mirror is only one wheel diameter forward of the rear wheel.

Add shading or color. Get the wheel wells nice and dark, and give emphasis to the dramatic side vent.

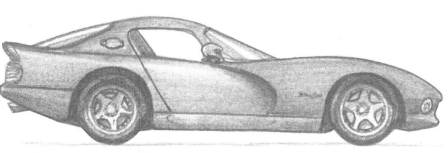

Shelby (AC) Cobra

Shelby Cobra is the American name for the AC Cobra, which has been produced on and off since 1962.

Draw the ground line. Using the wheel diagram above, draw the wheels the correct distance apart. Draw lines for the bottom of the vehicle, a shorter one for the bottom of the window, and a very light mark that indicates the top of the windshield.

Note that the windshield is a little more than one wheel diameter forward of the rear wheel. Add windshield, a bit more for the hood, and the head restraint.

Add the little "wind wing" (air deflector) to the A-pillar, and the louver , exhaust pipe, headlight and bumper. Draw the (easy!) wheels, and finish tires and wheel wells. Add the roll bar, side exhaust, vents, and other details.

Add shading or color.

The actual wheels you'll see on vintage Cobras are often spoke wheels, and very difficult to draw.

Always start out lightly!

The 2015 Corvette Z06 packs 650 horsepower, and earns its title as "Super Corvette" or "Stingray on steroids."

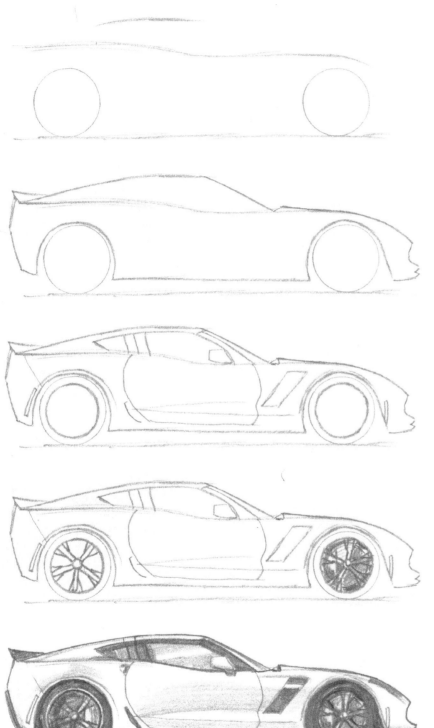

Draw the ground line. Using the wheel diagram above, draw the wheels the correct distance apart. Make a very light guideline above each wheel to establish height of the fenders, then draw the curving top profile.

Complete the overall shape of the car.

Add windows, more body lines, other details, and a circle inside the wheels for the rims.

The wheels consist of five spokes, but each is doubled, then doubled again. In this particular view, they don't really stand out. Draw the wheel rims.

And shading and color if you wish. Turn your paper as needed, and have a spare piece under your hand so it doesn't smudge your drawing.

BMW 318

The BMW 318 is a compact executive car produced from 1982 through 1991.

Draw the ground line. Using the wheel diagram above, draw the wheels the correct distance apart.

As always, use the wheels as a reference for placement of windows and pillars above. Draw lines for the bottom, front, and back of the car. Add slanted lines indicating the bottom and top of the windows.

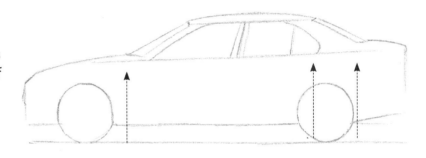

Using the wheels as a reference, draw the windshield, A-, B- and C-pillars.

Add details and start shading or coloring.

Notice the difference between the third and final drawing. Once you have basic shading done, get bold and make the darkest parts even darker!

Always start out lightly!

The Subaru XV Crosstrek was developed from the Subaru Impresa, with a higher ground clearance.

Draw the ground line. Using the wheel diagram above, draw the wheels the correct distance apart. Draw the basic body lines.

Complete the outline of the car body, including wheel wells. Outline the windows and pillars. Add the mirror.

Draw door outlines, handles, lights and other details you see. (Except the line off the hood that I need to erase.)

My wheel is not exactly accurate, but it captures the funky five-spoke pattern:
- draw two more circles (the rim);
- make five evenly spaced dots;
- over each dot, make a little "house;"
- outline the space inside and add a few more details.

Now finish by carefully shading when your pencil is dull, and sharpening lines and edges when it's sharp.

Smart ForTwo

When they say "ForTwo," they mean it! The Smart car was introduced in 2009. This is a 2013 model. Though it looks as though it could be squashed like a bug, it has a surprisingly strong "cage" frame, and does well in crash tests.

Draw the ground line. Using the wheel diagram above, draw the wheels the correct distance apart. Draw the basic body lines. Look carefully—they're unusual!

Add basic body lines and circles for the wheel rims.

Add more body detail and add another circle for the inside of the rim, and another in the center.

Each has twelve spokes, which sounds scary until you do some basic math: 12/3=4. So make four evenly spaced dots on the tire (which will become dark and hide them), then add two more between each. Now it's easy to draw twelve evenly-spaced spokes. (Unless, like me, you end up moving the center dot. I was pretty much able to cover up my error in the front wheel.)

Carefully add shading or color.

Always start your drawing lightly!

2016 Volkswagen Beetle

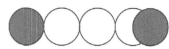

In the last edition of Draw Cars, the newest vehicle was the 1998 New Volkswagen Beetle. For the 2015 edition, it will remain the newest vehicle.

Draw the ground line. Using the wheel diagram above, draw the wheels the correct distance apart. Draw the basic body lines.

Add curves and shapes for the front and back. Add the slope behind the passenger area. Outline wheels and wheel wells.

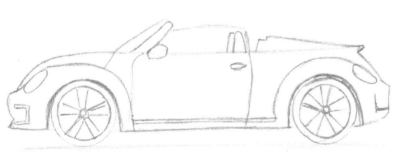

Add more details: curved fender lines leading to ovals for lights, door lines, and beginnings of the five-spoke wheels. Though simple in design, they can be difficult to get right (as I demonstrate)!

In fact, they're still not perfect in the final drawing, but the addition of strong shadows and shading means they con't draw as much attention.

Add shading and sharpen key lines, such as the outline and the fenders.

The one millionth old VW beetle was built in 1955 (see page 60). When production stopped in 2003, 21.5 million of them had been built.

1906 Franklin

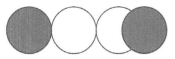

My, how times change! The earliest automobiles had plenty of clearance underneath to handle rough roads. On a long drive, this car might average 25 mph (40 km/h).

The Franklin Automobile Company manufactured cars between 1902 and 1934 in the United States. It was a luxury brand.

Draw the ground line. Using the wheel diagram above, draw the wheels the correct distance apart. Add a line for the bottom of the windows.

Draw the basic body lines. As you can see, the proportions are completely different than what we're used to seeing! When you have everything in place, shade the dark underside and wheel wells.

Don't forget the rear-view mirror! *(What rear-view mirror?)*

Add shading or color.

Always start out lightly!

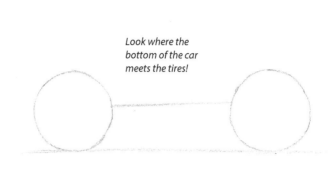

Look where the bottom of the car meets the tires!

Look where the front and rear meet the tires!

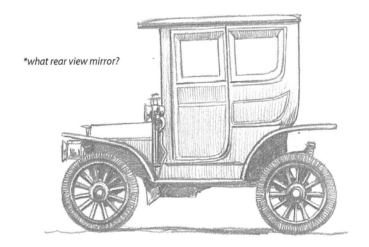

*what rear view mirror?

Always start out lightly!

Introduced in 1932, the Ford Model B replaced the boxier Model A. This version had a fold-out "rumble seat" in the back for extra passengers, and became popular for making custom hot rods.

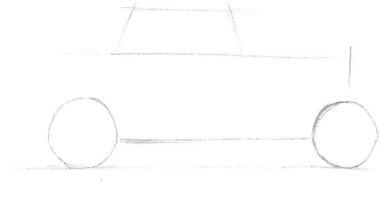

Draw the ground line. Using the wheel diagram above, draw the wheels the correct distance apart. Notice where the bottom of the car meets the tires! Draw lines for the basic shape and proportion of the body.

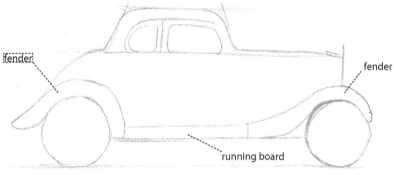

fender

fender

running board

Add the curving fenders. Turn your paper upside-down to draw the back of the front fender. Add the curving back end, and round the top of the passenger compartment. Add more lines to the windows.

rumble seat

Draw the bumpers, spare tire, rumble seat, and louver (ventilation slats) on the side of the engine compartment. No need to carefully count the spokes — notice how they almost disappear with shading.

Add shading or color.

Henry Ford wrote in his autobiography about the first production-line cars: "Any customer can have a car painted any color that he wants so long as it is black."

1946 Chrysler Town and Country

This upscale post-World War II vehicle featured hand-crafted wood side panels. The intricacy of that construction makes this a difficult car to restore — not many people have the skills and equipment.

Draw the ground line. Using the wheel diagram above, draw the wheels the correct distance apart. Draw light lines to indicate the bottom of the windows — actually lower than the hood (bonnet) in front and trunk (boot) in back.

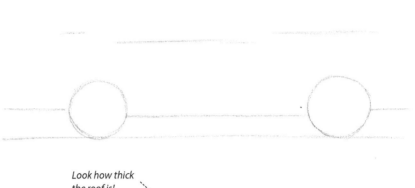

Draw the rounded rear end, front end, curved roof, windshield, and windshield visor.

Look how thick the roof is!

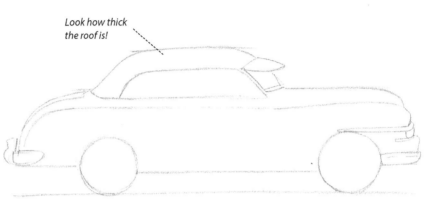

Eek! Lots of lines and details! Take your time —it will be worth it. Add more circles for the wheel rims and hub caps.

Add shading or color.

I have a link to a photo of one of these beasts on our web site at drawboks.com/drawbooks/. It's worth checking out!

Always start your drawing lightly!

The 1961 Corvette featured a new "duck" tail. This was the last year the contrasting body side color was offered, an option that most buyers chose, which cost $16.15. The car itself cost $3,934.

Draw the ground line. Using the wheel diagram above, draw the wheels the correct distance apart. Draw the bottom body line, top body line, and a very light mark to indicate the height of the windshield.

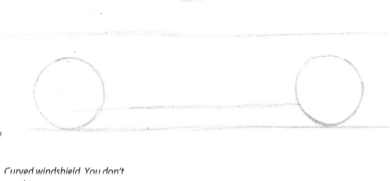

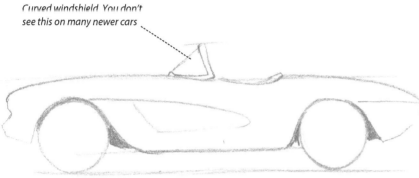

Curved windshield. You don't see this on many newer cars

Draw and darken the unusually-shaped wheel wells. Complete the front and back outline, then add the windshield and side panel.

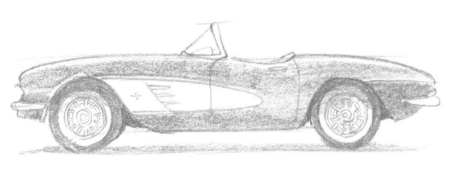

Draw more circles in the wheels and map out the 10-spoke wheel design. Erase lines you don't need and start shading.

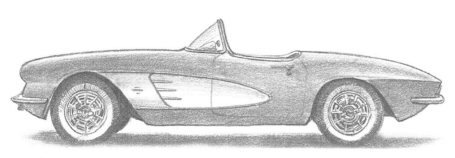

Comparing steps three and four, you can see what a difference it makes to pay attention to the state of your pencil. When it's sharp. go over lines and make them bolder and crisper. When it's duller, add shading.

1950s Fiat 500

In the 1950s, Americans started loving big, gas-guzzling cars to drive on their new highway system. In Italy, they needed small, fuel-efficient vehicles for driving in narrow, old city streets. The Fiat 500 served both needs well with its 500cc 2-cylinder motorcycle engine. I see many of these still driving where I live in Uruguay. I always feel like I'm watching a cartoon when I see them.

Start with the ground line, carefully spaced wheels, and lines for the bottom of windows, and top of the roof.

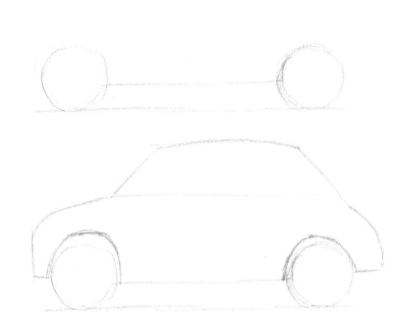

Complete the overall outline of the vehicle.

Outline door, hood, windows, and wheel wells. Add wheel rims with eight little spaces in each.

Add shading or color.

Looks like it should have a wind-up key sticking out the back! Fiat's current 500 is considerably larger, has an engine almost three times as big, and contains some of the most advanced technology found in a passenger car.

Always start your drawing lightly!

1959 Cadillac

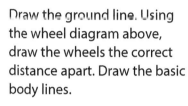

The 1959 Cadillac featured the most excessive "jet" tail fins ever made, with bullet tail lights. The tail fins had gotten larger every year since 1950.

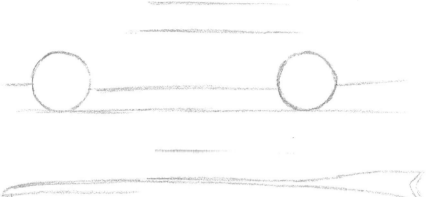

Draw the ground line. Using the wheel diagram above, draw the wheels the correct distance apart. Draw the basic body lines.

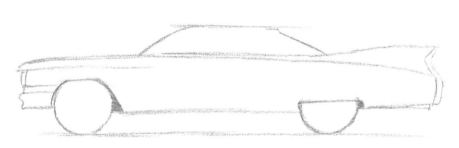

Complete the overall shape of the car, including the jet-fight-inspired tail fins. Add lines on the front fender.

Draw wheel wells

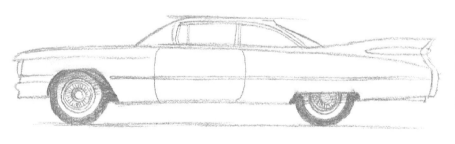

Draw the windows, door outline, taillight cowling, and side trim. Add details to the wheels and whitewall tires.

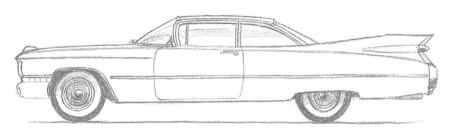

Do a few more details, clean up with your eraser, and you're done!

2015 Land Rover Defender

Rugged, four-wheel drive Land Rovers were first made in 1948. The brand has belonged to several companies. It currently belongs to the Indian company Tata. To commemorate the first drawing of a Land Rover, drawn in the sand, they drew one 1 km (.6 mile) long. You can watch the short video on landrover.com.

Draw the ground line. Using the wheel diagram above, draw the wheels the correct distance apart. Draw the basic body lines. Note the angles.

Add lines for windows, roof, b-pillar, and wheel wells.

Continue with lines for door, spare tire, head- and tail lights, body contours, and basic wheel design. You'll see each has six little triangles pointing inward, which then connect to one another.

Now continue to add shading and details. As always, work on fine lines and detail when your pencil is sharpest. As it gets dull, do shading.

Humvee

The United States Army contracted in the mid-1980s for a "High Mobility Multi-Purpose Wheeled Vehicle" to replace the aging Jeep. One requirement was a width that would allow it to follow in ruts of larger Army trucks. A civilian version was made from 1992 through 2010.

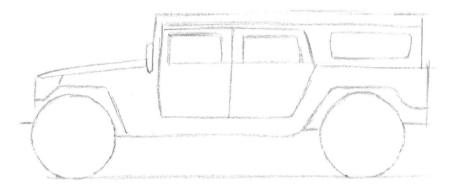

Draw the ground line. Using the wheel diagram above, draw the wheels the correct distance apart. Notice how high the bottom line is — great ground clearance! Mark where the bottom of the windows and top of roof will be.

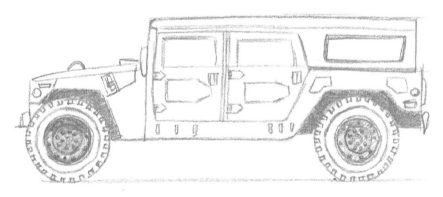

Draw door and window outlines, mirror, and other lines.

Add all kinds of details!

Shade or color.

Uncle Bill's Ratty Old Pickup

*Before you start, look carefully at your **reference material** (for now, my finished drawing).*

Draw the ground line. Using the wheel diagram above, draw the wheels the correct distance apart. Draw the bottom — notice how high it is off the ground! Add a line for the bottom of the windows.

Draw the outline of the cab and stylish slanting camper back.

Add the line between cab and bed of the truck, door outline, window outline, and line for trim running the length of the side. Add wheel rim details, darken the wheel wells, and shade the tires.

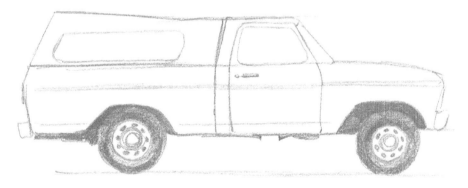

Add shading or color.

Uncle Bill thinks of this ratty, clunky, smoking old pickup truck as family. Which it is, sort of. Unfortunately.

Always start your drawing lightly!

But think of the possibilities!

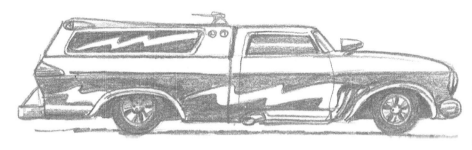

Maybe Uncle Bill will take it into the garage, get out his welding torch, chop and channel It, add some aircraft hydraulics, and make it into a screaming lowrider street rod!

Or maybe he installs a few dozen extra shock absorbers, raises the whole thing so high you need a stepladder to get in, then drops in an engine that shakes the ground like an earthquake.

Then again, maybe Uncle Bill's going to light up a quarter mile drag strip with a nitro-burning funny car so powerful it needs extra wheels behind to keep it from flipping over backward!

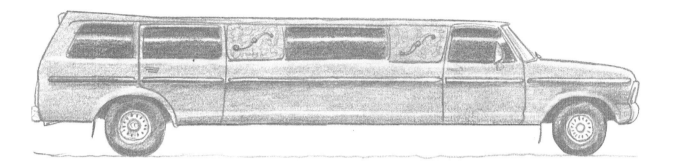

It may turn out that Uncle Bill is a very practical sort, saving to turn his ratty ol' pickup into a classy limo.

Then again, perhaps he lives a secret life as a undercover defender of democracy. He just wants you to think it's a ratty ol' pickup, when in fact he's ready for anything!

It's fun to think of the possibilities!

Perhaps you don't have an Uncle Bill.

(Do you have a bus driver?)

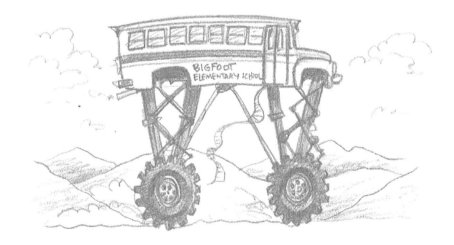

Part three: draw a car from an angle

In the next few pages, you'll look closely at a car from an angle. You'll learn how to draw the basic body parts and lines that shape the car—step by step.

Drawing a car at an angle involves perspective, which can be very pronounced, as in this street rod.

Or it may be barely noticeable, as in this vehicle, that appears to be viewed through a telescope.

Ford F-150

Drawing a car or truck from an angle is more complicated than drawing it from the side. Always use reference material.

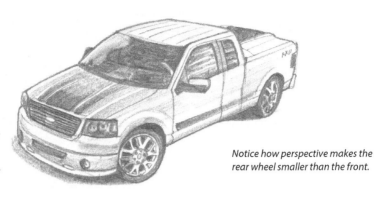

Notice how perspective makes the rear wheel smaller than the front.

For this drawing, your reference material will be this finished drawing. You can find a link to the original on drawbooks.com/drawcars).

It helps, many times, to think in terms of boxes in perspective. (If you're not familiar with perspective drawing, see my book *Draw 3-D*.) The pickup truck is basically a long box with a smaller one on top.

windshield slopes back

sides slope inward

front slopes back

Draw lines for the ground and top of the tires. Notice how they are not parallel —they get closer together as they go toward the distance.

Add ovals (ellipses) for the wheels. Take care to space them properly.

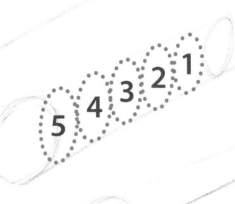

Add a line of the bottom of the truck.

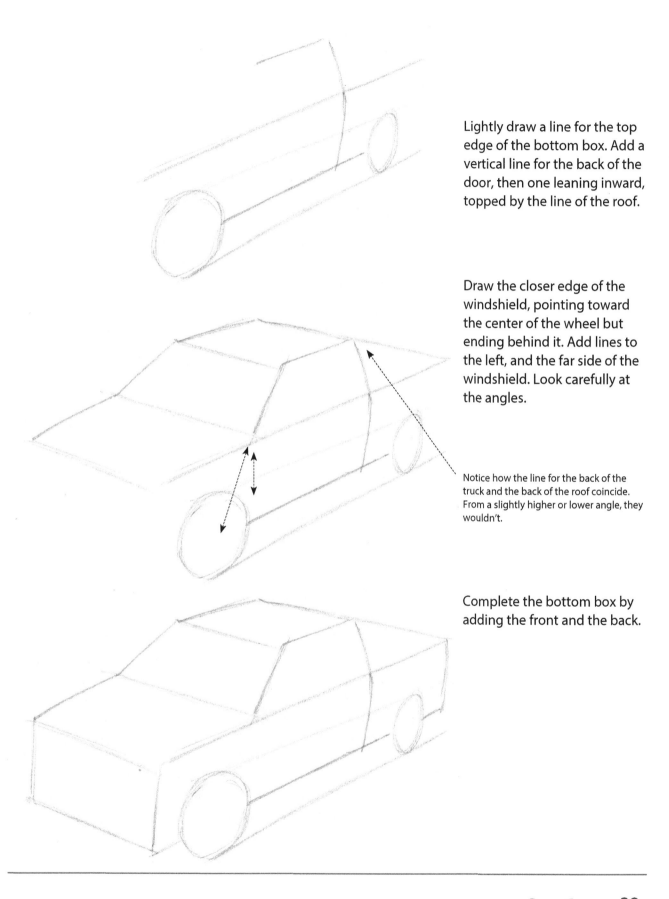

Lightly draw a line for the top edge of the bottom box. Add a vertical line for the back of the door, then one leaning inward, topped by the line of the roof.

Draw the closer edge of the windshield, pointing toward the center of the wheel but ending behind it. Add lines to the left, and the far side of the windshield. Look carefully at the angles.

Notice how the line for the back of the truck and the back of the roof coincide. From a slightly higher or lower angle, they wouldn't.

Complete the bottom box by adding the front and the back.

Erase the bottom line of the front of the bottom box, and make it a curve. Turn your paper upside-down and put a piece of scrap paper under your hand so you don't smudge the part you've already drawn.

scrap paper to protect your drawing

Draw a similar, but angled, line connecting the tops of the headlights and grill.

Indicate the bottom of the headlights and grill.

Add more details and ellipses (ovals) for lights in the front.

Draw all the lines you want to include before you start shading.

The wheel looks particularly complicated, but identify the pattern and you can see that it's based on six repetitions. Once you identify the dominant element (in this case, the largest open area), you can start with three of them evenly spaced, and add the other three between them, or you can work form the six dots for lug nuts.

Then add a little shading or color. OK, a lot of shading or color.

About Perspective

Perspective comes into play every time you draw a car from an angle.

Sometimes — as in the case of this 1959 Cadillac — the effects are very noticeable. If you draw the basic body lines, you'll see they extend back to a single vanishing point.*

The wide-angle lens on the camera makes this photograph more dynamic.

Here you can see a Mercedes-Benz M-class sport utility vehicle with a similar "wide-angle" view. Because of the dramatic wide-angle view, it looks as though it's ready to leap into action, perhaps in hot pursuit of a Pachycephalosaurus.**

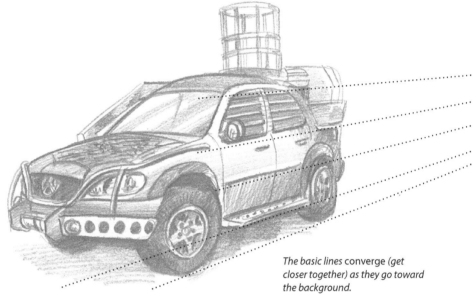

The basic lines converge (get closer together) as they go toward the background.

With a telephoto lens, this advertising photo gives a different impression: the vehicle looks much less wild. Probably just as well; there's not much of a market for cars to chase dinosaurs.

* for more on perspective, see my book *Draw 3-D*

** this vehicle was actually introduced to the public in the movie. For more on Pachycephalosaurus, see *Draw Dinosaurs.*

Part four: more cars from an angle

Surprise!

The cars pictured here don't appear in Part Four! Use them as reference material, and you can draw them using what you learned in Part Three.

BMW Z3

Always start out lightly!

The first mass-marketed BMW, the Z (for Zukunft, "future" in German) 3 was manufactured from 1992 through 2002, when it was replaced by the Z4.

Note the primary angles, displayed in the clock face.

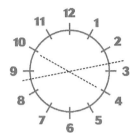

Start with the ground line and the wheels. Add the basic body lines.

Draw lines to show depth, on the rear deck, front, and windshield. Look at the clock face if you find the angles confusing. Add the distinctive curves of the hood.

With all these lines in place, add more details.

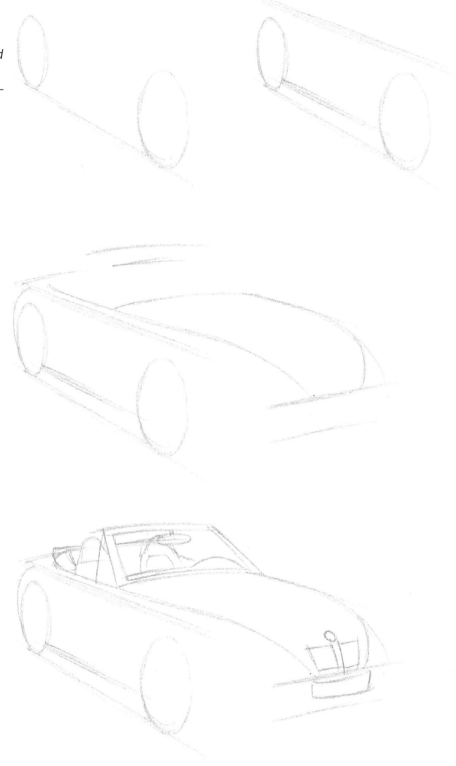

Always start your drawing lightly!

Finishing the drawing takes the most effort, so make sure you're happy with your drawing so far.

Look at it in a mirror, or hold it up to the light and look at it through the back of the paper. Does everything look right, forward and backward?

If not, ask yourself what you can fix to make the drawing look better. Start over if you need to.

When you're satisfied with the angles and proportions, add more details. Add details while your pencil is sharp. Add shading when your pencil is dull. If you have more than one pencil, use a softer one (3B) for shading and a harder one (HB) for details.

Look again at the final drawing. Add any details you've missed.

Porsche 918 Spyder

Always start out lightly!

A mid-engined plug-in hybrid supercar designed by Porsche, the Spyder is powered by a 4.6 liter V8 engine, developing 608 horsepower, with two electric motors delivering an additional 279 horsepower) for a combined output of 887 horsepower. Top speed is around 340 km/h (210 mph).

Start with a ground line and wheel well curves. Draw the rectangle (in perspective) above. Note that this is roughly the cockpit to the back of the car. Because of its curves, there is no outside edge above the wheels.

Now roughly add the windshield, and make light marks indicating the top and bottom of the headlights.

The headlights give you a reference for the curve of the far fender and front. To draw the latter, turn your paper upside-down. Using the windshield as a reference point, draw the double cowling and door line.

Add more to the front.

Always start out lightly!

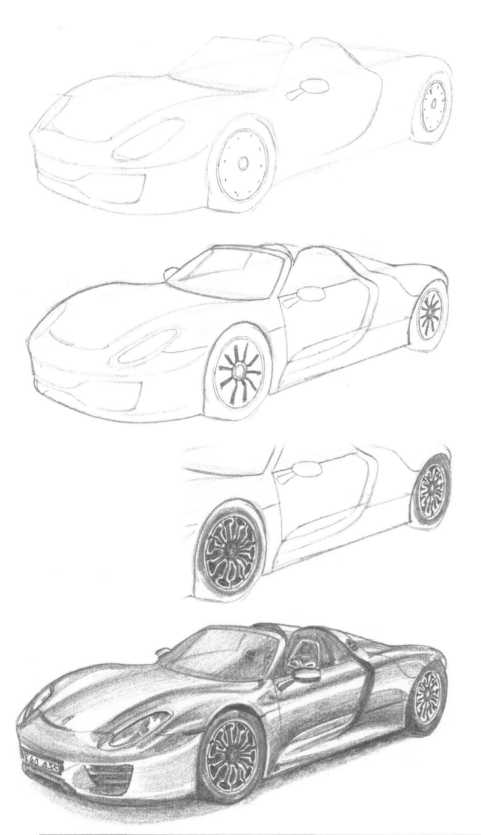

Now to tackle the wheels! This is where an ellipse template comes in very handy. Here I've used the template to draw an oval, and drew the one inside freehand. I have to do this because I want to the rim to remain light. Carefully place ten dots for spoke guides: two opposite one another, and four in between. Draw an oval for the center of the wheel.

Make another oval around the center, and draw black lines almost to the rim — almost because you want a tiny white space. Note how a few of them curve slightly. Add more lines showing the body contour. The one from the cowling to the rear wheel well does this especially nicely.

At the end of each black line, near the rim, add a little "paddle," still not touching the innermost oval of the rim. Fill in between each, leaving a white space.

Add a little shading (LOL!) and other details.

If you can, I highly recommend you look at the original, a gorgeous photo of an amazing vehicle. You can find a link on our web site drawbooks.com/drawcars.

Mahindra Bolero Attitude

The Bolero Attitude is, a customized version of the Bolero VLX, which Indian car maker Mahindra introduced in 2010.

Draw the lines pointing toward the vanishing point (of the edge of the paper). Add the vertical lines and ovals. Try to make it look just as weird as this one!

Sketch lines for the hood (bonnet), bumper, and roof, and mark where the right front wheel will be. Note that the line of the hood forms a straight line with the line on the side. This means it's at eye level. Having it tilted for effect makes it look like it's turning to go uphill.

Add wheel wells and the trim above them (notice I didn't add the back of the front one until the final step). Draw more front details. Always look carefully at where one piece is in relation to another. For example, the line of the windshield points to the closer side part of the bumper, and the first opening of the grill is directly above that.

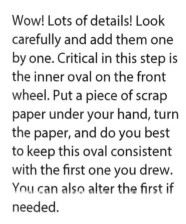

Wow! Lots of details! Look carefully and add them one by one. Critical in this step is the inner oval on the front wheel. Put a piece of scrap paper under your hand, turn the paper, and do you best to keep this oval consistent with the first one you drew. You can also alter the first if needed.

Wow again! Even more details! If you can, work from the original photo. You can find a link to it on our web site: drawbooks.com/draw-cars. Notice the pick strapped to the side near the rear wheel (it has a shovel on the opposite side). The wheel has a five-spoke design with some extras.

Shade (or color; no doubt you can find a more attractive color then the original's orange).

Remember to turn your page, put a piece of scrap paper underneath your hand to prevent smudging, and be aware of the sharpness of your pencil. Dull is good for shading, while sharp is good for lines.

Plymouth Prowler

The Plymouth Prowler, later the Chrysler Prowler, is a "retro" styled production car built in 1997 and 1999-2002 by DaimlerChrysler.

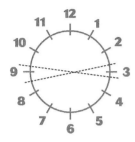

Not many cars come to a point in the front, so the Prowler presents an interesting challenge.

Draw the ground line, the wheels and the basic body lines.

Draw the curved lines that form the pointed front of the car. Add the windshield and back body line. Again, look at the clock face if you find the angles confusing.

Add the other front wheel, the two-part bumper and fenders.

Always start out lightly!

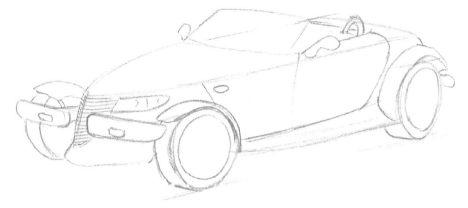

Continue adding details. Pay careful attention to angles, and look at your drawing in the mirror or from the back (if you can see through the paper) to spot any problem area.

When you're satisfied with the angles and proportions, add more details and shading. Add details while your pencil is sharp. Do shading when it's dull. If you have more than one pencil, use a softer one (3B) for shading and a harder one (HB) for details.

Remember:
- Turn your drawing as you work Use a piece of scrap paper to keep your hand off finished parts.
- Clean up any smudges with your eraser. Make sure all final lines are crisp and sharp.

Add remaining details and shade or color your vehicle.

Formula 1 Racer

Always start out lightly!

Formula One is the highest class of single-seat racing cars. Each car must follow specific rules, hence the word formula. They travel at speeds up to 360 km/h (220 mph). This one is from the 1990s.

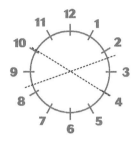

This vehicle appears as if viewed from a distance. The lines leading into the distance are almost parallel.

Draw the ground lines, the wheels, the basic body lines, and in this case the top of the air scoop.

Add the rounded point of the front of the car, the rim of the cockpit, and the cowling that covers the engine.

Look at the shape of the car! Check the clock face if you find the angles confusing.

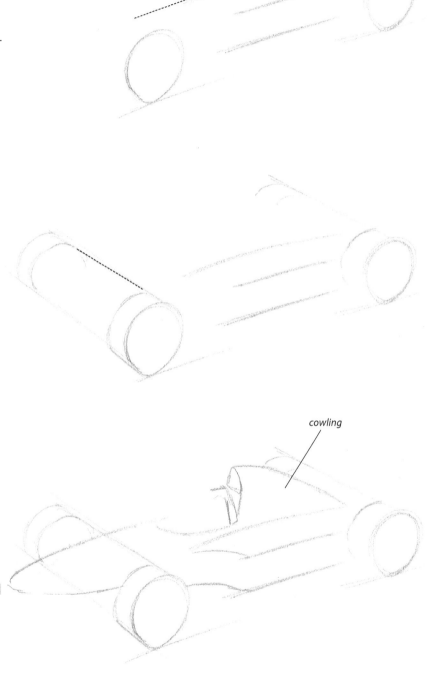

cowling

Always start out lightly!

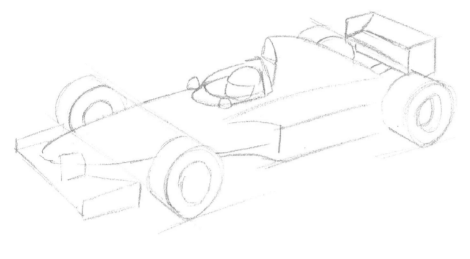

Finishing the drawing takes the most effort, so make sure you're happy with your drawing so far.

When you're satisfied with the angles and proportions, add more details. Add details while your pencil is sharp.

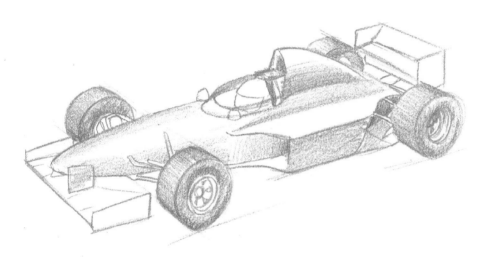

Add shading when your pencil is dull. If you have more than one pencil, use a softer one (3B) for shading and a harder one (HB) for details.

Look again at the final drawing. Add any details you've missed.

Of course, this Formula 1 car is unlike any you'll actually see, since it's not covered in advertising from the sponsors.

Also, the newer ones have gotten positively weird looking. Do your own image search to see how the design of Formula 1 cars has changed over time!

1957 Chevy

The '57 Chevy is one of the most popular and sought-after classic collector's cars.

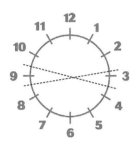

In terms of perspective, this telephoto view of a relatively box-like car presents no particular challenges.

Draw the ground lines, the wheels, and the basic body lines. Add the distinctive headlights.

Draw lines showing depth on the front of the car and windshield. Look at the clock face if you find the angles confusing. Add the rear end line and flaring wheel wells.

Add the curves of the windshield, side trim, front bumper, and other details you see.

Always start your drawing lightly!

Finishing the drawing takes the most effort, so make sure you're happy with your drawing so far. Look at it in a mirror, or hold it up the light and look at it through the back of the paper. Does everything look right, forward and backward?

If not, ask yourself what you can fix to make the drawing look better. Start over if you need to.

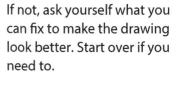

When you're satisfied with the angles and proportions, add more details and shading. Add details while your pencil is sharp. Do shading when it's dull. If you have more than one pencil, use a softer one (3B) for shading and a harder one (HB) for details.

Turn your drawing as you work Use a piece of scrap paper to keep your hand off finished parts.

Clean up any smudges with your eraser. Make sure all final lines are crisp and sharp.

Stand back and admire your creation!

T Bucket Street Rod

Always start out lightly!

This popular street rod (a hot rod that is legal to drive as a normal car) takes its inspiration from the Ford Model T, built between 1908 and 1927.

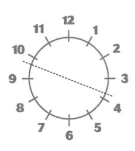

In this view, the lines of the side of the car present no particular challenge ...

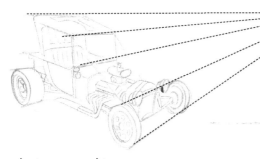

... but you need to pay particular attention to the vanishing point of the other lines!

Draw the side wheels, and the basic body lines.

Draw lines for the windshield, and to show depth on the side, front, and top of the car. Draw guide lines to find the correct placement of the other front wheel. Add additional ellipses to add depth to the wheels.

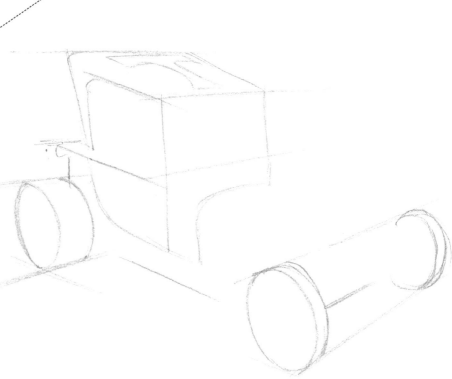

Always start out lightly!

When you get to this point, take time to look at your drawing in the mirror, or through the back of the paper. Does everything look right?

When you're satisfied with the angles and proportions, add more details and shading.

Remember:
- Turn your drawing as you work Use a piece of scrap paper to keep your hand off finished parts.
- Clean up any smudges with your eraser. Make sure all final lines are crisp and sharp.

Funny Car

Funny cars are drag racing vehicles designed to look like normal cars. Unlike dragsters, funny cars have the engine in front, and its size is limited.

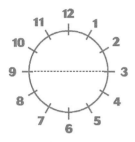

Draw the ground line and the wheels.

Note that the ground line is horizontal. Also, the rear wheel is very much larger than the front.

Look at how the bottom of the car lines up with the bottom of the front wheel, and with the middle of the rear wheel. Draw the body lines.

Add depth lines on the front of the car and windshield. Draw the fenders overlapping the wheels.

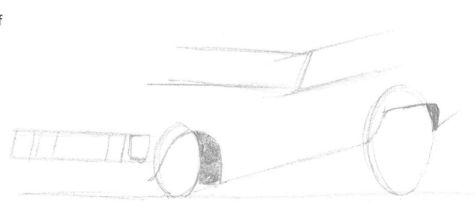

Always start your drawing lightly!

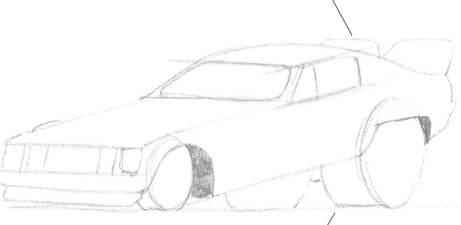

The rear spoiler is made of aluminum and magnesium and capable of producing 5,000 pounds of downward force on the rear tires.

Draw the rest of the outline of the vehicle. Add the spoiler. Draw the second rear wheel, and add depth to the front one.

The rear "slicks" are 18 inches wide, nearly ten feet in circumference, and inflated with only four pounds pressure!

When you're satisfied with the angles and proportions, add more details. Add details while your pencil is sharp.

Look again at the final drawing. Add any details you've missed. As with the Formula 1 racer, a funny car will most likely be covered in advertising.

Stand back and admire your creation!

The gallery

Here's a weird collection of vehicles to give you ideas. Try drawing them!

A. Ford Model T - 1920s. Quite a leap from it to the T-Bucket on page 57!

B. 1933 Ford Model Y - British (note mirror on right, which is the driver's side)

C. 1950s concept car. Its tail fins put the '59 Cadillac (page 31) to shame!

D. 1,000,000th Volkswagen "Beetle" rolled off the assembly line in 1955

E. Exotic car called Isdera from an unusual angle, showing the slope of its side windows and size of its windshield.

A

B

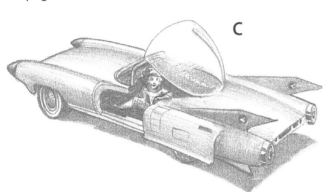

C

D

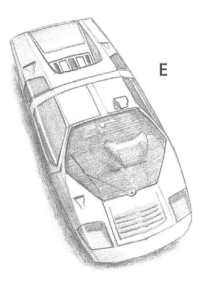

E

Always start out lightly!

F

G

F. A concept car called the Ethos, exhibited at a car show in the hope of selling the design to a car manufacturer.

G A prototype minivan that I don't think ever made it into production.

H. Lamborghini Countache – compressed perspective from photo (on the side of a model box!) taken with a telephoto lens.

I. Landrover from a similar angle – interesting comparison to the Lamborghini!

J. Mazda racing prototype. I used to drive one …

… *just kidding!*

H

I

J

Tips and Tricks: Wheels from an Angle

Although I have a template for ellipses, I don't usually use it. I prefer to draw freehand.

These photos show how the ellipses go together to make a wheel from an angle.

Starting with a horizontal and vertical line, draw one ellipse. Next, slide the template along the horizontal line, and draw part of a second ellipse, the same size as the first.

Use a ruler to connect them to make the top and bottom of the tire. Now slide the template to the right, slightly beyond the first vertical line, and make a smaller ellipse.

Though you don't have to, you can add another, still smaller ellipse on the same vertical axis. Then slide the template left to the first vertical line for the rim of the wheel.

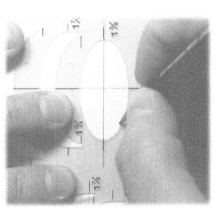

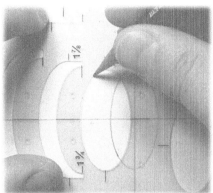

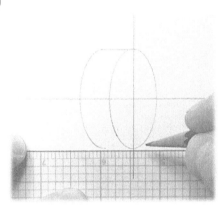

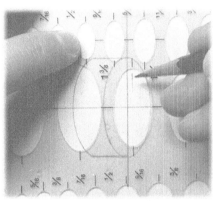

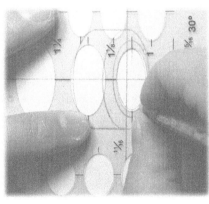

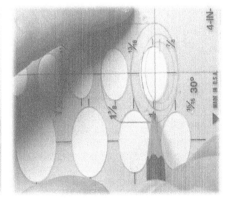

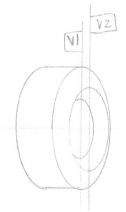

V1: vertical axis used for largest and smallest ellipse
V2: vertical axis used for in-between ellipse

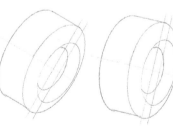

When viewing wheels from above, rotate the axes. Note that they remain perpendicular to each other.

Always start out lightly!

Tips and Tricks: Imagination!

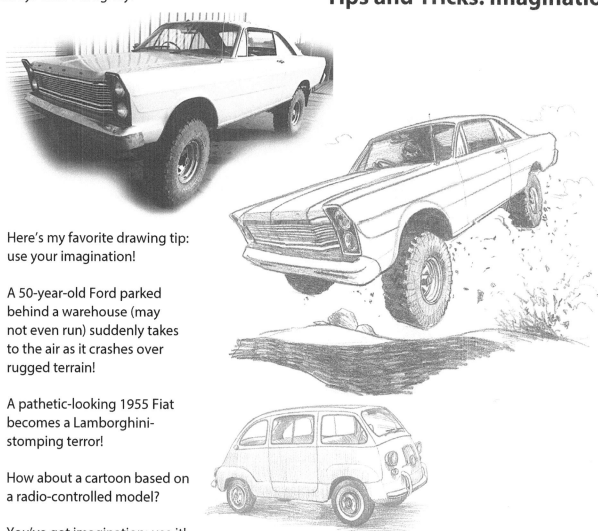

Here's my favorite drawing tip: use your imagination!

A 50-year-old Ford parked behind a warehouse (may not even run) suddenly takes to the air as it crashes over rugged terrain!

A pathetic-looking 1955 Fiat becomes a Lamborghini-stomping terror!

How about a cartoon based on a radio-controlled model?

You've got imagination: use it!

OOPS...

WHO'S LAUGHING?

LAMBORGHINI

Have you enjoyed this book?

We'd love a review on Amazon or your favorite retailer's web site!

Remember, you can find frequently-updated cars reference material (photos) and inspiration on our Pinterest feed. Check it out:

drawbooks.com/drawcars

Find other titles in this series online at drawbooks.com